Topic 1
Macroeconomic performance

The recent macroeconomic performance of the UK

Macroeconomics is concerned with the economy as a whole, in contrast to microeconomics which is concerned with how the component parts of the economy work. Macroeconomics focuses on such issues as economic growth, inflation, unemployment and the balance of payments. The macroeconomic performance of the UK, since 2000, can be assessed in relation to the government's key macroeconomic objectives. These can include the following:

- economic growth
- inflation
- employment/unemployment
- the balance of payments

1 **Assess the macroeconomic performance of the UK since 2000. (AO2)** **8 marks**

....

....

....

....

Economic growth

Short-run and long-run

It is important to distinguish between short-run and long-run economic growth:

- Short-run refers to actual growth. This is where there is a movement from within a production possibility curve to a position on a production possibility curve.
- Long-run refers to potential growth. This is where there is a shift in the production possibility curve to the right, providing an increase in the productive potential or productive capacity of an economy.

The contrast between actual growth and potential growth can be seen in Figure 1. The movement from *A*, within the production possibility curve, to *B*, on the production possibility curve, indicates actual economic growth. The movement from *B* to *C*, outside the original production possibility curve PPC_1, but on PPC_2, indicates potential economic growth.

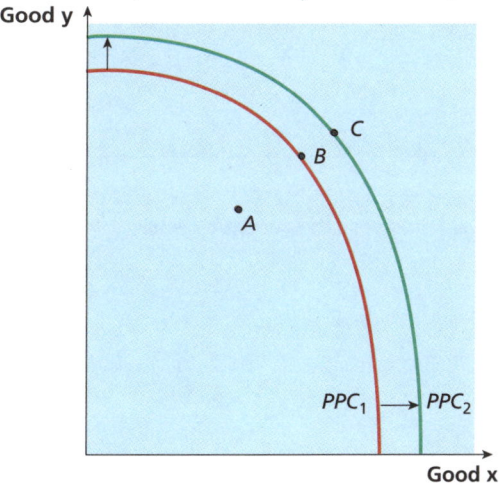

Figure 1 The contrast between actual growth and potential growth

Deviation from trend growth and output gaps

The long-run trend rate of growth will be influenced by the different stages of the trade cycle (Figure 2). This is also known as the business cycle or the economic cycle.

These stages are referred to as:
- boom
- recession
- slump
- recovery

A boom is the phase of the economic, trade or business cycle in which economic growth is at its most rapid. As the recovery in the economy improves, economic growth becomes faster until it is growing at a rate that is unsustainable in the long run.

A recession is the downswing in the economic, trade or business cycle. It is during this phase of the cycle that aggregate demand may begin to decline. Business confidence will be low, so investment is likely to be falling. The technical definition of a recession is two successive quarters of negative growth. The most severe recent depression in the world was in 2008–09.

A slump is the low point of the economic cycle. At this phase in the cycle, aggregate demand is well below the level of full-capacity output in an economy.

A recovery is the upswing phase of the cycle when aggregate demand and output begin to rise, although this is likely to be at a slow pace to begin with.

The long-run trend is generally shown as a straight line in a diagram, but an economy is most likely to be at a point above or below this straight line and only occasionally actually on the line. It is possible to see whether the long-run trend of growth deviates from what would generally be expected of it.

An output gap shows the difference between the actual output and the potential output of an economy when it is working at full capacity. It is possible to look at changes in real GDP over a period of time and compare these with the long-run trend rate of growth to see if there is a deviation or divergence. This output gap can be either positive or negative.

Figure 3 shows both a negative and a positive output gap. Points A and D are on the long-run trend line, but points B and C are below this trend line. Between A and D, below the long-run trend line, there is a negative output gap.

Beyond point D, the actual GDP line is above the long-run trend line, e.g. at points E and F. Between points D and G, above the long-run trend line, there is a positive output gap.

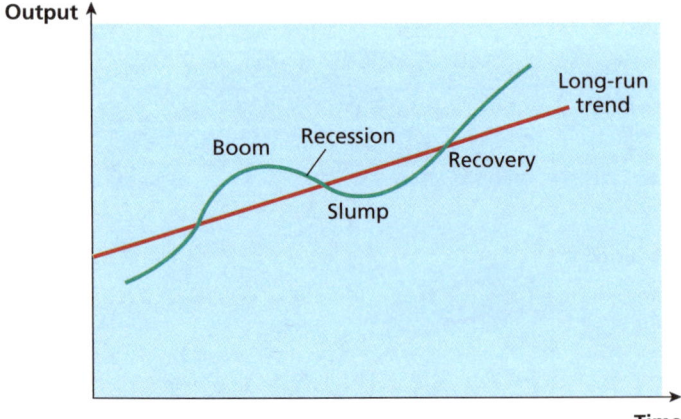

Figure 2 The trade, business or economic cycle

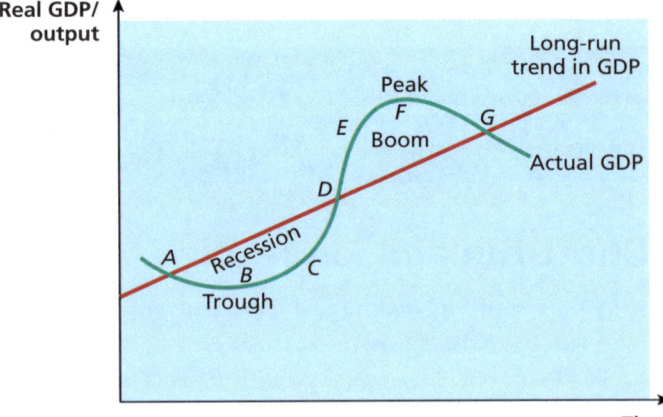

Figure 3 The output gap

2 Analyse the difference between short-run and long-run economic growth. (AO3) `12 marks`

....

....

....

....

....

....

....

....

....

....

....

....

....

....

....

....

....

....

....

....

....

....

....

3 Explain what is meant by the 'economic cycle' or 'trade cycle'. (AO2) `6 marks`

....

....

....

....

....

....

....

....

....

....

....

④ Analyse the nature and significance of an 'output gap'. (AO3)   12 marks

....

....

....

....

....

....

....

....

....

....

....

....

....

....

....

....

....

....

....

....

....

Causes of economic growth

It is important to distinguish between short-run and long-run causes of economic growth.

Short-run causes of economic growth

Short-run causes of growth include the following:
- increases in aggregate demand
- increases in short-run aggregate supply
- the interaction of the multiplier and the accelerator
- the economic cycle

Increases in aggregate demand and aggregate supply can contribute to economic growth, but it is also necessary to understand the importance of the multiplier and the accelerator.

The multiplier refers to the amount by which an increase in injections into the circular flow of income will increase the level of total income in an economy. These injections can be in the form of investment, government spending or exports. The size of the multiplier will depend on the extent to which these injections into the circular flow of income leak away as withdrawals from the circular flow of income, in the form of savings, taxation or imports.

The size of the multiplier in an economy can be calculated in the following way:

$$\frac{1}{MPS + MPT + MPM}$$

MPS = marginal propensity to save; MPT = marginal propensity to tax; MPM = marginal propensity to import.

The accelerator refers to the relationship between investment and the rate of change of output in an economy. It is not just the change in output that is important, but the rate of change. The effect of this relationship is that investment is likely to fluctuate more than output.

The size of the accelerator in an economy can be calculated in the following way:

$$I = f(\text{change in } Y)$$

This means that investment is a function of the rate of change in national income.

The interaction between the multiplier and the accelerator is important in explaining the cyclical changes that can occur in an economy. For example, an increase in investment during the upswing of the economic cycle will have a multiplier effect in the economy, leading to a larger increase in income.

As the economy approaches full capacity, the accelerator theory stresses that investment will fall, creating a downward or negative multiplier effect. Eventually there will be a need for investment to grow. There is thus an economic cycle that is continually repeating itself.

Long-run causes of economic growth

Long-run causes of growth include the following:
- increases in long-run aggregate supply
- increases in the quantity and quality of the labour force
- increases in capital stock

Long-run aggregate supply will be relatively elastic to begin with, as output grows, but as the availability of resources becomes increasingly limited, long-run aggregate supply becomes increasingly inelastic until it eventually becomes a vertical line.

However, it is possible in the long run to change the quantity and/or quality of resources. This would allow the long-run supply curve to shift. For example, over time, the labour force can increase, especially as a result of net migration into a country. The quality of a labour force could also be increased as a result of a government's supply-side measures, such as providing training courses to enhance the skills of workers, making them more employable.

The capital stock can also be changed in terms of quantity and/or quality in the long run. For example, replacement capital will be able to take advantage of technical progress and innovation, making the equipment more effective and cost-efficient.

---

5 **Define the national income multiplier and explain what determines its size. (AO2)** **6 marks**

....

....

....

....

....

....

6 **Explain the interaction of the 'multiplier' and the 'accelerator'. (AO2)** **6 marks**

....

....

....

....

....

....

Exam-style question

7 **Evaluate the causes of economic growth in both the short run and the long run. (AO4)**

Consequences of economic growth

Economic growth can have a number of consequences for an economy. It can affect the following:

- inflation
- employment/unemployment
- the balance of payments
- the government's fiscal position

Economic growth can be regarded as favourable for an economy. An increase in the value of the output produced in an economy can be expected to lead to an increase in the level of unemployment, although the actual effect will depend on the extent to which the additional output has come about through labour-intensive, rather than capital-intensive methods of production.

Growth can be favourable for a country's balance of payments too, although the actual effect will depend on the extent to which the additional output is exported.

Growth can also be beneficial to a country's fiscal position. For example, if growth leads to a reduction in unemployment, the government will gain by paying out less money on unemployment benefits and receiving more money from taxation payments, both direct and indirect.

Growth, however, may not have such a positive effect on the rate of inflation in a country. If there is economic growth, and more people are employed, this could increase the level of aggregate demand, creating demand-pull inflation. If the reduction in unemployment pushes up wages, this could lead to cost-push inflation.

8 **Discuss the consequences of economic growth for an economy. (AO4)**　　20 marks

Continue writing on the next page.

[Ruled note-taking space]

Policy issues

The role of fiscal, monetary and supply-side policies

Fiscal, monetary and supply-side policies have a key role to play in relation to the promotion of a number of areas of an economy, including the following:

- economic stability
- economic growth
- international competitiveness

The role of policy rules, targets and constraints

In the promotion of these areas of the economy, however, there will be a number of possible restrictions on freedom of action, including the following:

- policy rules, e.g. fiscal rules
- targets, e.g. inflation targeting
- constraints, e.g. policy trade-offs

An example of one of these restrictions is the need for a government to seek to achieve a particular objective. In the UK, the government aims to keep the rate of inflation to no more than 2% per annum, as measured by the consumer price index. If the rate of inflation reaches 3% or above, the governor of the Bank of England is formally required to write a letter to the chancellor of the exchequer, explaining why the rate of inflation is 1% or more above the target for this policy objective. This acts as a restraint on the government, for example in relation to policies to bring down the rate of unemployment, which in August 2013 was 7.8%.

In July 2013, the rate of inflation reached 2.9%, very close to the figure that would require the governor of the Bank of England to write a letter to the chancellor of the exchequer. In this situation any expansion of aggregate demand, in an attempt to reduce the rate of unemployment, might not take place for fear of taking the rate of inflation to 3% or over. This illustrates the potential trade-off in terms of achieving different macroeconomic objectives, such as simultaneously achieving a low rate of inflation and a low rate of unemployment. This link between changes in inflation and changes in unemployment is shown in the Phillips curve.

9 **Explain how fiscal, monetary and supply-side policies can affect the international competitiveness of an economy. (AO2)**

6 marks

10 **Analyse the significance of the restrictions that can apply to government macroeconomic policies. (AO3)**

12 marks

Topic 2
Trade and integration

Absolute and comparative advantage

The advantages of international trade are based on the theories of absolute and comparative advantage.

Absolute advantage

The theory of absolute advantage is based on the idea that if one country has an absolute advantage in the production of certain products, i.e. it can produce them using fewer resources and therefore at a lower unit cost than another country, then it should specialise in the production of those products. It is, therefore, sometimes also described as 'absolute cost advantage'.

Comparative advantage

The theory of comparative or relative advantage, however, is based on the idea that even if a country has an absolute advantage in producing everything, there may still be a reason for another country to produce some products.

The reason for this is that if one country is not the best at producing anything, it can still benefit from specialising in the production of something that it is relatively good at producing, in comparison to other goods. A country will specialise in the production of that product in which it has the lowest opportunity cost and then trade it with other countries.

This is another example of the importance of opportunity cost in the study of economics, as the theory of comparative advantage is based on differences in opportunity cost ratios between various countries.

1 **Analyse the difference between absolute and comparative advantage. (AO3)**   12 marks

Alternative exchange rate systems

There are several alternative exchange rate systems. The most common type is the floating or flexible exchange rate system — exchange rates are determined in the foreign exchange market by the forces of demand and supply, just like any other price in a market.

The demand for, and the supply of, a currency will be influenced by a number of factors, including:
- the demand for goods and services
- savings in different financial institutions
- changes in interest rates in different countries
- speculation on the likely future value of a currency

The demand for goods and services from different countries will result in demand for currencies to pay for these.

It is not only goods that are moved from one country to another. It is possible to deposit savings in a variety of different financial institutions in various countries. Switzerland, for example, has long been an accepted place to deposit savings. Deposits of money in particular accounts in various institutions are influenced by a number of different factors, but one of the most important of these is the reward that is paid in the form of an interest rate. Money can be moved to take advantage of differences in interest rates in various

countries. Money moved around in this way is known as 'hot money'.

At the other extreme is the fixed exchange rate system — a government decides on the value of the exchange rate and then intervenes in the market by buying or selling the currency on a regular basis to maintain this rate. A government will need to maintain extensive foreign reserves to allow it to intervene regularly.

The advantage of this approach is that businesses have a degree of certainty when planning as the exchange rate will be known in advance (unless there has been a devaluation or a revaluation of that exchange rate) and there is no speculative pressure on the currency to move up or down. The disadvantage, however, is that the government must have the funds available to intervene in the foreign exchange market to support the currency if this becomes necessary.

Another type of exchange rate system is the managed or dirty float. This is a combination of the other two systems. The exchange rate floats, but the government intervenes, when it thinks that the rate is getting too high or too low.

---

7 **Explain how exchange rates are determined in different exchange rate systems. (AO2)**

6 marks

....

....

....

....

....

....

....

....

....

....

....

....

....

Exam-style question

8 **Evaluate why a floating exchange rate system is often preferred to a fixed exchange rate system. (AO4)**

20 marks 40

....
....
....
....
....
....
....
....
....
....
....
....
....
....
....
....
....
....
....
....
....
....
....
....
....
....
....
....

Exchange rate fluctuations

Fluctuations in the exchange rate come about just like that of any other price in a market, i.e. as a result of changes in demand and supply.

Exchange rate fluctuations can have a number of consequences for an economy. For example, if the value of an exchange rate in a floating system falls, or depreciates, it will have the effect of reducing the price of exports. This could help the current account of a country's balance of payments if the demand for these exports is elastic. But there is no guarantee that a lower price will cause the demand for exports to increase because demand is affected by a number of possible factors, not just price.

At the same time, a depreciation in the value of an exchange rate will have the effect of increasing the price of imports. If the demand for imports was price elastic, this would be likely to reduce the demand for them, but there is no guarantee that this will be the case. If the demand for imports is inelastic, the increased prices of the imported goods will simply contribute to an increase in the rate of inflation. This will apply to both the prices of the finished goods that are imported and the prices of the domestically produced goods which include a high proportion of raw materials and component parts that are imported from abroad.

9 Describe the possible causes of exchange rate fluctuations. (AO1)   4 marks

10 Analyse the consequences of fluctuations in the exchange rate for an economy. (AO3)   12 marks

Purchasing power parity

Purchasing power parity refers to the attempt to compare standards of living in different countries by taking into account the price levels in the different countries. Exchange rates are adjusted in order to give comparisons between different countries which take into account purchasing power in different countries. The idea is that an amount of money in one currency can be exchanged for an amount of money in another currency, but both will be able to purchase the same basket of products.

The human development index, for example, takes into account comparative living standards through figures for gross national income (GNI) per capita that have been adjusted to take account of purchasing power parity. This recognises that without such an adjustment, it will not be possible to make effective comparisons between standards of living in different countries, given that price levels may vary significantly between them.

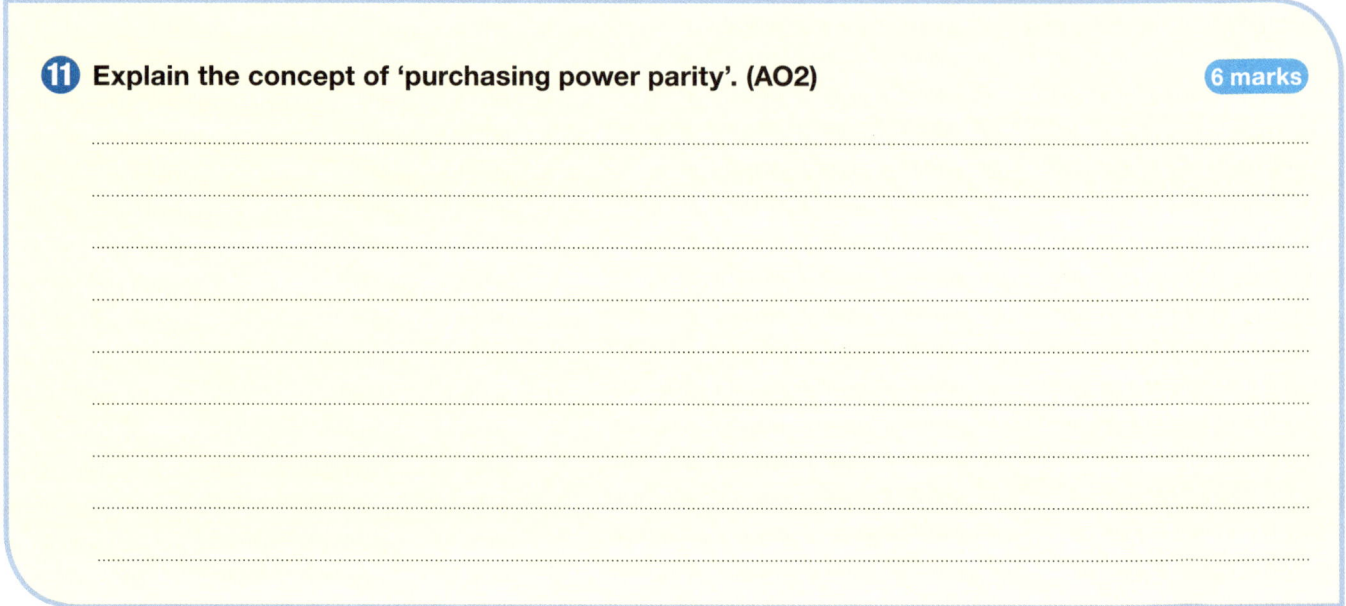

11 **Explain the concept of 'purchasing power parity'. (AO2)**　　　　6 marks

Causes and consequences of balance of payments problems

Balance of payments problems can come about as a result of various causes. The main reason, in terms of the visibles, is that the value of the imports coming into a country is greater than the value of the exports leaving a country. The term 'visibles' refers to actual goods that are traded, i.e. something that is tangible.

A macroeconomic objective is to achieve stability in the balance of payments over a number of years, i.e. with the number of deficits being broadly equal to the number of surpluses. This is not always easy to achieve,

however, and persistent deficits in the current account of the balance of payments can have a number of negative consequences for an economy. Various policies can be used to correct such imbalances.

Only a small number of countries have regularly managed to achieve a surplus in the current account of their balance of payments. They include Switzerland, China, Germany and Japan. The majority of countries have a deficit in their current accounts. The severity of these deficits can be judged by the ratio of the deficit to GDP (Table 2).

Table 2 Current account deficit (or surplus) for selected countries as a % of GDP in 2013

Country	Current account balance as % of GDP
Switzerland	7.9
China	6.0
Germany	5.0
Japan	2.8
UK	−1.7
USA	−2.7
Spain	−5.5
Sweden	−7.7
Bulgaria	−9.8
Greece	−10.9

12 Describe the possible causes of balances of payments problems. (AO1) `4 marks`

13 Analyse the consequences of balance of payments problems for an economy. (AO3) `12 marks`

Policies to correct imbalances

One way to reduce a deficit in the balance of payments is to adopt protectionist policies that are designed to reduce the number and value of imports coming into a country.

A number of methods of protection can be used to reduce imports, including:

- tariffs
- quotas
- subsidies
- import licences
- administrative regulations
- exchange controls
- embargoes

One of the problems with the adoption of protectionist methods such as these is that they can lead to retaliation, i.e. if import controls are imposed on a particular country, that country may also impose import controls to reduce the goods coming into it. If this happens, nobody is then able to take advantage of the potential gains from trade arising from specialisation and comparative advantage.

Arguments in favour of protectionism are usually based on the protection of particular industries. These can include infant (or sunrise) industries that are just beginning to be established, and declining (or sunset) industries that are experiencing a fall in demand and need to be allowed to decline slowly so as to avoid a large increase in unemployment. Protectionism can also sometimes be used to protect key or strategic industries in a country, such as agriculture and the production of military weapons. A further reason relates to 'dumping' — this is when products are sold in a country not just cheaply, but below the cost of production in the exporting country.

Arguments against protectionism, however, are based on the idea that it goes against the theory of comparative advantage, denying consumers the potential benefits from greater levels of production all over the world.

---

14 **Discuss which would be the best policies to correct imbalances in the balance of payments. (AO4)**

20 marks

15 Analyse the differences between a tariff and a quota. (AO3)   `12 marks`

16 Discuss the cases for and against protectionism. (AO4)

Stages of economic integration

There are various stages in the process of economic integration, including:

- **Free-trade area.** In this form of integration a group of countries promote free trade among themselves, but each member keeps its own set of trade barriers against other countries.
- **Customs union.** Like a free-trade area, this encourages free trade among the member countries but, unlike free-trade areas, it imposes a common external tariff against products from countries outside the union.
- **Single market.** In this form of integration there is an attempt to establish a unified market, providing for the free movement of goods, services and people.
- **Economic union.** The member countries agree to use the same economic policies and regulations.
- **Monetary union.** Countries agree to use a common currency. The countries in the European Union which are part of the eurozone are an example of this form of integration.

There are many examples of economic integration in the world today, including:

- **European Union (EU).** The European Union can trace its origins to the creation of the European Economic Community in 1958 when it comprised France, Germany, Italy, the Netherlands, Belgium and Luxembourg. The UK joined in 1973. It now consists of 28 countries, 17 of which have adopted a single currency, the euro. The UK is one of 11 countries in the European Union that has decided to retain its own currency.
- **North American Free Trade Agreement (NAFTA).** NAFTA consists of three countries: the USA, Canada and Mexico. It is a free-trade area, but each of the three countries retains its own barriers on trade with countries outside the Free Trade Agreement.
- **Association of South East Asian Nations (ASEAN).** This association was established in 1967 with five members: Thailand, Indonesia, Malaysia, Singapore and the Philippines. It has gradually grown in size over the years and now consists of 10 countries. The five additional countries are Brunei, Cambodia, Laos, Myanmar and Vietnam.

17 **Explain the stages of economic integration. (AO2)** `10 marks`

Continue writing on the next page.

23

18 **Describe one example of economic integration. (AO1)** `4 marks`

Impact of economic integration

It is possible to separate the impact of economic integration into short-run and long-run effects.

- **Short-run: trade creation (internal) and trade diversion (external).** Economic integration can lead to both trade creation, where member countries benefit from the free trade that now exists, and trade diversion, where some countries will suffer as a result of the integration. It is important that these two effects of integration are understood because it is usually the case that whenever some form of economic integration takes place, there will be both gainers and losers.

- **Long-run: dynamic effects.** The long-run effects of integration can be dynamic, arising from the increasing interdependence between different economies and the greater degree of harmonisation of regulations. This is why there has been an increase in the number of examples of economic integration, and even where there have been problems, such as in the European Union, the number of members continues to grow.

19 **Evaluate the possible impact of economic integration. (AO4)**

20 marks

Evaluate the possible impact of economic integration. (AO4)

20 marks

Topic 3
Development and sustainability

Meaning and measurement of development

In order to understand development, it is necessary to take into account the following:
- the relationship, and the distinction, between growth and development
- gross domestic product (GDP) per capita
- human development index (HDI)
- economies at different stages of development
- common and diverse characteristics

Growth and development need to be clearly distinguished. Economic growth refers to an increase in real output over a period of time, usually measured through changes in real GDP.

Development is a broader concept that takes into account more than just the material standard of living in a country. For example, it could also include life expectancy and education. The human development index (HDI) goes beyond GDP per head. There is now an even broader measure of development, called the multidimensional poverty index.

Michael Todaro identified the most important characteristics of developing countries as the following:
- low standards of living, typified by low levels of income, a high level of inequality of wealth and income, poor health and inadequate education
- low levels of economic productivity and efficiency
- high rates of population growth
- a high dependency ratio
- a high level of dependence on the primary sector of production, especially agriculture
- a high level of dependence and vulnerability in international trading, such as in movements in the terms of trade

The economist W. W. Rostow identified five stages in the process of development. These are:
- the traditional society
- the transitional stage
- the take-off
- the drive to maturity
- the stage of high mass consumption

Rostow argued that all countries tended to experience a similar sequence of development, characterised by these five stages.

The human development index has already been referred to. This was an attempt, first established in 1990, to look at development using more criteria, going beyond real GDP per capita. The HDI examines the progress of countries in terms of three criteria:
- the standard of living
- life expectancy
- education

---

1 Distinguish between 'growth' and 'development'. (AO1)　　　　　　　　　**4 marks**

2 Explain the relationship between 'growth' and 'development'. (AO2)

6 marks

....

....

....

....

....

....

....

....

....

Exam-style question

3 Analyse why HDI is considered to be a better measure of development than GDP per capita. (AO3)

12 marks 24

....

....

....

....

....

....

....

....

....

....

....

....

....

....

....

....

....

....

....

....

....

4 Analyse the common and diverse characteristics of economies at different stages of development. (AO3)

`12 marks`

....

....

....

....

....

....

....

....

....

....

....

....

....

....

....

....

....

....

....

....

....

....

....

....

Policies to promote economic development

There are a number of possible policies to promote economic development. These involve:
- the role of the market
- the role of the state
- international trade
- economic integration

It is often argued by economists that market forces should always be encouraged because this brings about greater competition in a market, leading to greater levels of efficiency. This is why privatisation is often supported.

There is often the possibility, however, that market forces can give rise to market failure and this is why the state will often intervene to help promote development. For example, there may be an under-provision of merit goods and no provision at all of public goods, and so the state may need to intervene to provide both types of goods.

There may also be elements of information failure where decisions are taken by people who are not in possession of all the relevant information to make an informed judgement.

The state may also be required to control and monitor monopolies to ensure that they are not operating against the public interest by using their power to provide a product at a price higher, and in quantities lower, than would be the case in a situation of perfect competition.

The importance of international trade and economic integration has already been considered.

5 Evaluate the effectiveness of policies to promote economic development. (AO4)

Evaluate the effectiveness of policies to promote economic development. (AO4)

The constraints on development

There are likely to be a number of constraints on economic development in a country. These could include:

- resource endowment
- infrastructure
- institutions
- finance and savings
- international constraints

These influences on the process of development can be extremely significant. For example, in terms of resource endowment, countries may be able to benefit from the location of factors of production within their geographical boundaries, such as oil in Saudi Arabia and diamonds in South Africa.

In terms of infrastructure, it is important that a country has a good system of transportation and communication and is able to benefit from satisfactory energy supplies. Pakistan, for example, is facing extreme difficulties in relation to the supply of electricity — this gives rise to power being turned off at regular intervals, a process known as 'load-shedding'.

Institutions are also vital in the development process. The existence of a stock exchange, for example, can be crucial in providing a way of raising capital.

The financial structure can also be an important influence on the process of development. For example, a country needs to have a sophisticated financial system in order to provide customers with the confidence to make deposits of money which can then be lent out to firms, so financing investment.

This is why the credit crunch of 2007–09 had such a significant effect on economies all over the world. The difficulties of raising finance contributed significantly to the economic recession that happened to most countries in all parts of the world.

6 **Discuss the relative importance of the different constraints on a country's economic development. (AO4)**   20 marks

The meaning of sustainability

Sustainability is an important concept in economics and to appreciate its meaning it is necessary to consider the following impacts of growth:

- social
- environmental
- resource
- demographic

Sustainability refers to the need of the present generation to take into account the potential effects of decisions taken today on future generations. For example, a greater emphasis should be placed on renewable, in contrast to non-renewable, resources. A reduction of carbon dioxide emissions would be another way of bringing about sustainable development in a country.

One of the best definitions of sustainability came from the World Commission on Environment and Development in 1987: 'Sustainable development is development that meets the needs of the present without compromising the ability of future generations to meet their own needs.'

The World Bank, in 1994, stated that economic growth 'brings with it the risk of appalling environmental damage. Alternatively, it could bring with it better environmental protection, cleaner air and water, and the virtual elimination of acute poverty. Policy choices will make the difference.'

7 Explain what is meant by 'sustainable economic development'. (AO2)   6 marks

8 Analyse the social, environmental, resource and demographic impacts of growth at different stages of development. (AO3)   12 marks

The measurement of sustainability

It is important to understand the uses and limitations of various economic indicators in measuring sustainable economic development, including:
- gross domestic product (GDP)
- index of sustainable economic welfare (ISEW)

GDP measures the value of all that has been produced within the geographical boundaries of a country over a given period of time, usually a year.

The ISEW was developed in 1989 and was designed to replace GDP because of the latter's limitations. For example, GDP did not take into account the distribution of income or the possible external costs associated with production.

The ISEW addresses these issues by taking into account income distribution and the various costs associated with production, including pollution and sustainability costs such as the environmental costs associated with habitat loss, depletion of non-renewable resources and climate change.

It also takes into account social costs, especially those associated with crime, divorce, commuting and unequal income distribution. In addition, it takes into account certain health costs, such as those associated with accidents on the road and in the workplace.

9 **Explain the uses and limitations of such indicators as GDP and ISEW in measuring sustainable economic development. (AO2)** **6 marks**

....

....

....

....

....

....

....

Policies and agreements to promote sustainability

A variety of policies and agreements can be adopted to promote sustainability. They can be seen in the context of three levels:
- **Regional policies.** These can apply to local communities and the producers and consumers in those communities. For example, recycling projects can exist at the local and regional level. The conservation of water and the use of solar panels are other examples.
- **National policies.** At the national level, the government can take an initiative in supporting nationwide policies, such as controls on pollution.
- **International agreements.** At the international level, agreements have been reached to encourage sustainable development, such as within the European Union. The European Commission has stated that 'sustainable development is an overarching objective of the European Union: we need to ensure that our present development does not compromise the ability of future generations to meet their needs'.

10 Evaluate the usefulness of national and international policies and agreements in promoting sustainability. (AO4)

20 marks

Topic 4
The economics of globalisation

The characteristics and consequences of globalisation

It is important to understand the different characteristics of globalisation, the factors promoting globalisation and the possible consequences of globalisation.

The International Monetary Fund has identified four essential features of globalisation:
- trade and transactions
- capital and investment movements
- migration of people across national boundaries
- the dissemination of knowledge

Globalisation stresses the interdependence of economic, social and cultural activities. The emphasis is on the connectedness of the world's economies. International economic and business activities are now much more common than in the past and there has been an increase in the number of multinational companies operating in the world. Globalisation stresses that economics does not recognise national boundaries and that competition is crucial to the achievement of the maximum level of efficiency in economic activity throughout the world.

1 **Describe the different characteristics of 'globalisation'. (AO1)**　　4 marks

2 **Explain the factors that promote 'globalisation'. (AO2)**　　6 marks

International financial flows

These can be categorised as follows:
- private
- official
- short term
- long term

3 **Analyse the influences on, and the effects of, the different flows of international finance. (AO3)**

12 marks

....
....
....
....
....
....
....
....
....
....
....
....
....
....
....
....
....

Nature and impact of multinational firms; foreign direct investment (FDI)

It is necessary to have an understanding of the nature and the impact of multinational firms, especially in relation to foreign direct investment (FDI).

A multinational is not simply a firm which *sells* in more than one country. To be classified as a multinational, a firm needs to *operate* in more than one country. For example, a firm could have manufacturing plants in different countries in the world. Such a firm would not just be selling in more than one country, it would actually be producing in more than one country. Japanese car companies, such as Honda, Nissan and Toyota, are examples of multinational firms because these companies have factories that produce cars in various countries. For example, each of these companies has factories in the UK: Honda in Swindon, Nissan near to Sunderland and Toyota near to Derby.

A multinational company is a good example of what could be described as 'footloose capitalism'. This means that it is becoming easier to move production from one country to another to take advantage of different factor endowments in various parts of the world, especially as these endowments affect the costs of production. This illustrates the idea of responding to market forces in order to enhance the prospects of profit maximisation.

4 Describe what is meant by a 'multinational firm'. (AO1)

4 marks

5 Explain what is meant by 'foreign direct investment'. (AO2)

6 marks

Exam-style question

6 Evaluate the impact of multinational firms. (AO4)

20 marks 40

Continue writing on the next page.

The role and impact of international financial institutions

There are three particularly important international financial institutions:

- **The World Trade Organization (WTO).** The WTO was established in 1995. Its main purpose is to monitor and regulate international trade. Its objective is to reduce trade barriers as much as possible so as to encourage free trade. Its website states: 'The World Trade Organization deals with the global rules of trade between nations. Its main function is to ensure that trade flows as smoothly, predictably and freely as possible.' It is involved in a series of discussions to achieve its objective. The current round is called the Doha Round, which has been taking place since 2001. The WTO now has 159 member countries.
- **The International Monetary Fund (IMF).** The IMF was established in 1947. Its main purpose is to coordinate the international monetary system. Its objective is to ensure the stability of the world monetary system and to provide financial support, if required. Its website states: 'The IMF promotes international monetary cooperation and exchange rate stability, facilitates the balanced growth of international trade, and provides resources to help members in balance of payments difficulties or to assist with poverty reduction.' It now has 188 member countries.
- **The World Bank.** The World Bank was also established in 1947. Its aim is to provide finance to those countries that need it, especially developing economies. Loans are sometimes conditional on a country's government adopting certain economic policies. The World Bank is made up of five organisations:
  - the International Bank for Reconstruction and Development (IBRD)
  - the International Development Association (IDA)
  - the International Finance Corporation (IFC)
  - the Multilateral Investment Guarantee Agency (MIGA)
  - the International Centre for Settlement of Investment Disputes (ICSID)

7 Explain the role and impact of (i) the World Trade Organization, (ii) the International Monetary Fund and (iii) the World Bank. (AO2) **9 marks**

....

....

....

....

....

....

....

....

....

....

....

....

....

8 Explain why some countries are reluctant to accept assistance from international organisations, such as the IMF or World Bank. **6 marks**

....

....

....

....

....

....

....

International trade negotiations and trade disputes

There are always likely to be issues surrounding current international trade negotiations, sometimes leading to trade disputes. These tend to involve the World Trade Organization in particular. For example, the Doha Round of trade negotiations has been going on since 2001.

The statement from Doha is as follows:

We shall continue to make positive efforts designed to ensure that developing countries, and especially the least-developed among them, secure a share in the growth of world trade commensurate with the needs of their economic development. In this context, enhanced market access, balanced rules, and well-targeted, sustainably financed technical assistance and capacity-building programmes have important roles to play.

9 Discuss the issues surrounding current trade negotiations. (AO4)   `20 marks`

Philip Allan, an imprint of Hodder Education, an Hachette UK company, Market Place, Deddington, Oxfordshire, OX15 0SE

Orders
Bookpoint Ltd, 130 Milton Park, Abingdon, Oxfordshire OX14 4SB
tel: 01235 827827
fax: 01235 400401
e-mail: education@bookpoint.co.uk

Lines are open 9.00 a.m.–5.00 p.m., Monday to Saturday, with a 24-hour message answering service. You can also order through www.hoddereducation.co.uk

© Terry Cook 2014
ISBN 978-1-4718-0001-6
First printed 2014
Impression number   5   4   3   2   1
Year   2019   2018   2017   2016   2015   2014

Cover photo reproduced by permission of Fotobank kiev/fotolia
Printed in Dubai

Hachette UK's policy is to use papers that are natural, renewable and recyclable products and made from wood grown in sustainable forests. The logging and manufacturing processes are expected to conform to the environmental regulations of the country of origin.

P02279

ISBN 978-1-4718-0001-6